Updated Edition

101 ways to rock in® LinkedIn

Updated Edition

Rock your personal brand to grow your network and grow your business!

VIVEKA VON ROSEN with
dayna steele

101 WAYS TO ROCK: LINKEDIN Updated Edition

PRINTED IN THE UNITED STATES OF AMERICA

PUBLISH DATE MARCH 2021

ISBN: 9798701209686

Publisher contact and book orders:

Daily Success Publishing
www.therockbusiness.com

To everyone who has suffered through the tumult of 2020 – and survived.

—Viveka von Rosen

OTHER BOOKS BY VIVEKA VON ROSEN

LinkedIn Marketing: An Hour a Day

LinkedIn: 101 Ways to Rock Your Personal Brand

101 WAYS TO ROCK BOOK SERIES

101 Ways to Rock Running for Office

101 Ways to Rock Everyday Activities for Success Every Day (Update)

101 Ways to Rock Solo Female Travel

101 Ways to Rock Online Travel

Havana: 101 Ways to Rock Your World

LinkedIn: 101 Ways to Rock Your World

In the Classroom: 101 Ways to Rock Your World

Welcome to College. 101 Ways to Rock Your World

On the Golf Course: 101 Ways to Rock Your World

OTHER BOOKS BY DAYNA STEELE

Rock to the Top: It Now Goes to Eleven!

Surviving Alzheimer's with Friends, Facebook, and a Really Big Glass of Wine

Rock to the Top: What I Learned about Success from the World's Greatest Rock Stars

Personal branding is the conscious and intentional effort to create and influence public perception of an individual by positioning them as an authority in their industry, elevating their credibility, and differentiating themselves from the competition, to ultimately advance their career, increase their circle of influence, and have a larger impact.

—Wikipedia

WHY YOUR PERSONAL BRAND MATTERS

The year 2020 forced us to pivot, to understand the importance of our business and our personal brand, and to learn how to create virtual business. Not only has business changed, so has the entire world. So many more of us are working from home and/or are creating new home-based businesses. That means it's even more important to create a strong personal brand, so you stand out from your competition.

In 2017, I merged my company with those of three other LinkedIn and Social Selling experts. In three short years, the new company, Vengreso, is now one of the foremost digital sales transformation companies helping solopreneurs to enterprise multi-nationals bridge the gap from in-person engagement and selling to remote selling and the creation of stronger personal branding on LinkedIn. With 2020 being what it was, it was time for an update to our original *101 Ways* book on best use practices for LinkedIn.

Reid Hoffman, co-founder and former LinkedIn CEO once said, "The fastest way to change yourself is to hang out with people who are already the way you want to be." In the past four years, I have grown even more enamored of the co-creator of this book, Dayna Steele. (#girlcrush). She is someone who makes a difference in this world. Why is this important? When you create your personal brand, you start with the bigger picture in mind. Who do you need to be to do what you want to do in the world?

Over the years I have sold used cars (really), managed a business office (not well), and tried several other businesses (with success but not much interest). In 2006, at an in-person networking event (remember those?), I was introduced to the business social media platform, LinkedIn. It caught my attention and, finally, my passion. What I saw was an extremely useful business tool and a way to create a powerful personal brand. The more I learned about using LinkedIn, the more I wanted to share it with other professionals.

Creating a powerful brand is a little bit business strategy and a little bit law of attraction. I created my brand on LinkedIn and then worked passionately to prove it true. Only then did I become an international *Forbes* recognized speaker on the subject of personal branding.

I saw LinkedIn was the perfect business tool for marketing and wrote, LinkedIn Marketing: An Hour a Day. Soon I was traveling the world to teach and talk about LinkedIn. (Pre COVD-19, obviously.) As my value grew as a top social media influencer (Forbes, four years in a row), I realized LinkedIn was a powerful tool for personal branding.

Vengreso co-founder Mario Martinez, Jr. says, "Your LinkedIn profile is NOT a resume. It is a buyer centric resource your prospects will utilize as a tool in their buying decisions." My new methodology is reflected in this updated version, *101 Ways to Rock LinkedIn*.

It starts with your foundation and mindset. Why are you creating your brand?

Once you have created your brand then what? You must learn to engage and then connect to your audience.

Once connected you will want to feed them the right content, and, finally, do it regularly with a cadence that helps you create more conversations with your connections, and convert them into clients and customers!

When I wrote the first version of this book in 2016, there were less people online. People were still discovering social networks. TikTok and Clubhouse did not yet exist. Today, every businessperson understands the need not only to create an online brand, but the necessity of standing out in this ever increasingly crowded space.

Your personal brand is how you appear to the world. Tom Peters first wrote about personal branding in the 1997 article, "The Brand Called You." Peters pointed out regardless of age, regardless of position, regardless of the business we happen to be in, all of us need to understand the importance of branding. We are CEOs of our own companies: Me Inc. To be in business today, our most important job is to be head marketer for the brand called You.

You are your brand. Whether you are an entrepreneur, jobseeker, sales professional, or corporate employee, you can still define your brand within your business, no matter what that business is.

LinkedIn gives you the ability to not only be seen by the world but control how the world sees you. With, (at publish date), more than 720 million members in 200 countries and territories around the globe, LinkedIn gives you access to a network like never before. When utilized effectively, LinkedIn opens the door to people, jobs, news, updates, and insights that will increase your odds of success substantially.

The key phrase here, "when utilized effectively," is why we wrote this book. LinkedIn is a powerful tool and a free one as well. Though there are paid services, most of what you can do for your own success with LinkedIn isn't going to cost you anything other than your own time and effort. And, since we all know time is money, this book will help you best streamline your efforts and help you find all LinkedIn has to offer to grow your professional network.

This book is about YOU!

YOU have a great service or product. Let's make sure those 720 million members in 200 countries can find YOU on LinkedIn and understand YOU are the best. There are 101 helpful tips in this book that will do just that.

A book does not write itself. To succeed, like anything, it needs a network. Thanks to my business partners at Vengreso: Mario Martinez, Jr., Bernie Borges, Kurt Shaver, Stan Robinson, Jr. and the rest of my amazing team (over 36 people now – holy cow!) And, thanks to Dayna – I'm still not as cool as her, but I'm working on it!

VIVEKA VON ROSEN

www.linkedin.com/in/linkedinexpert

WHY YOU SHOULD ROCK YOUR BRAND

As a Texas rock radio Hall of Famer, I spent years on the radio in my hometown of Houston, Texas. From there I became an e-commerce entrepreneur, aerospace executive (long story), motivational business speaker, author of numerous success books, a business success coach, voiceover artist, Broadway investor, and a candidate for the US Congress (another long story).

After leaving radio, I put my personal rock brand behind me and began work to create a new one. I just assumed it was what I needed to do to be taken serious in business. It took me several years to realize the brand I had created during those rock and roll years *and* the lessons I had learned from rock stars and one-hit wonders were invaluable, not only to my business efforts, but to others as well. It was my memorable personal brand already to so many.

Now, I happily embrace my rock brand, using it to underscore the *Rock Star Principles* of success – podcasts, speeches, and books. It gives me the opportunity to work with rock stars in varied industries around the world. Rock stars like Viveka Von Rosen and you! And, I personally use every one of Viveka's tips and they have helped move my brand to the forefront over the years.

DAYNA STEELE
www.therockbusiness.com

101
ways
to
rock
in
LinkedIn

The buyer is always tuned in to one radio station: WIIFM (What's In It For Me). The rest is filtered out as noise.

—Steve Woodruff

1

Get Focused

Who are you? What do you do? Who do you do it for? What will they get out of it? If you aren't clear on the answers, take some time and talk to those who know you best. If you don't know who you help and how you help them, stop reading and come back when you do.

Someone who thinks they can help everybody, will end up helping nobody.

—Viveka von Rosen

2

Be Clear Who You Help

Clarity is key to personal branding. So, you must be clear on HOW you help others. The clearer you are, the more likely you are to convert your connections into conversations, and those conversations into customers.

Today you are You, that is truer than true.
There is no one alive who is Youer than You.

—Dr Seuss

3

Be Memorable

If you can tell a prospect how they benefit from buying your service or product, you become memorable. Using a cosmetics salesperson's pitch as an example, which one would you buy from?

I can help anyone with a face.

I help 40+ women present themselves to the public in their best and most youthful light.

The foundation for any marketing – content or otherwise – is your target audiences, buyer personas, customer profiles, industry segments – whatever you want to call this directed and in-depth research and depiction of who buys what from you and why.

—Ardath Albee

4

Write A Client Description

This isn't something you'll ever post on LinkedIn, but it helps establish who you are talking to in your own mind. Create a buyer persona of your typical buyer – age, gender, job, education and why they use you or your product. Imagining your buyer when writing your profile will make it convert better. Know your audience.

9:39

◂ Search

Skills & Endorsements

Online Marketing · 1,127

Blogging · 1,258

Content Strategy · 215

Social Media Marketing · 1,475

Marketing Strategy · 595

Consulting · 281

Entrepreneurship · 651

Social Media · 948

Marketing · 619

Public Relations · 419

Online Advertising · 227

Social Media Measurement · 221

SEO · 198

5

Create Your Own Keywords

When you create your list of keywords, think about the search terms people would use when Googling someone like you. Titles, industries, companies, names, locations, skills, products, and services are all keywords. Think verb, noun, acronym and synonym: accountant, CPA, accounting, book-keeping, QuickBooks.

The purpose of an elevator pitch is to describe a situation or solution so compelling that the person you're with wants to hear more even after the elevator ride is over.

—Seth Godin

6

Have A Good Elevator Pitch

Who do you help? How do you help them? Who are you, and what makes you different? Figure out what that is and learn to say it in one compelling sentence. Elevators are fast these days. Knowing how to do this is an important key to successful branding and to writing a good professional headline and audio intro.

If you can't explain it simply, you don't understand it well enough.

—Albert Einstein

7

Your Paragraph Pitch

Once you have someone's attention, expand on it even more by elaborating with a few more details. Who have you helped? What were their results? What can people expect from you? Three to five sentences for this paragraph is a good length. You'll use this later in the About section.

English Français 

English Default

Français 

How it works

We will match viewers' language to your available language profile. If there's no match, your default profile will be shown.

+ Add profile in another language

Create your profile in another language 

 Add more than one language on your profile to make finding you easier.

 We will match viewers' language to your available language profile. If there's no match, your default profile will be shown.

Language of new profile *

Choose...

8

What Languages Do Your Clients And You Speak?

LinkedIn allows you to replicate your profile in additional languages. If you serve an international clientele, create a profile in the languages of the clients you serve and the languages you speak. A definite plus to any profile.

The language, especially the vocabulary, peculiar to a particular trade, profession, or group: such as medical jargon.

—Dictionary.com

9

What Jargon Do Your Clients Regularly Use?

Marketing or sales prospects will expect to see words like ROI and KPI. The average person might not know what that means, but your ideal client knows what it is. Add relevant jargon to your keyword list and sprinkle those into various sections of your profile.

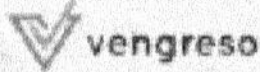

LinkedIn® Profile Template

Fill out each section to create a profile for yourself or your employees.

Viveka von Rosen
[illegible]

Name [illegible]	[illegible]
Username/PW Don't share with anyone!	
Email Address [illegible]	[illegible]
Profile Photo Add your photo or link to your photo here.	[illegible]
Cover Photo [illegible]	[illegible]
Headline [illegible] 120 Characters.	[illegible]
Summary/About [illegible]	[illegible]

10

Create Your Content In Word First

A good rule of thumb when creating content for LinkedIn (or really for anything), is to write it in Word first, and then check your spelling and grammar. Nothing says unprofessional like misspellings and bad grammar. For a professional and visually pleasing content, use white space, special characters, bullets, and capitalization.

It takes 20 years to build a reputation and five minutes to ruin it. If you think about that, you'll do things differently.

—Warren Buffett

11

Be Consistent In All Your Branding

Once you are clear on who you are, what you do and whom you serve, create relevant and consistent written copy, visuals, and shared content everywhere on LinkedIn – including your profile picture. If you claim to be a serious businessperson, don't share silly cat videos in your feed. You get the idea.

You never get a second chance to make a great first impression and your LinkedIn profile is your chance to make a great first professional impression.

—Ted Prodromou, LinkedIn Author and Speaker

12

Your Name

Seems obvious, but people really do mess up their names on LinkedIn. Double-check your spelling. And use your name and only your name. "John Doe: Master of the Universe" goes against LinkedIn's User Agreement. Don't add your area of expertise, telephone number, email address, or your call to action in the Name field. If LinkedIn catches you doing this, they might restrict or close your account.

Viveka (Vivica) von Rosen

Helping #SalesProfessionals Create More QUALIFIED & QUALITY Conversations | @LinkedInExpert & Speaker | Forbes Top 20 Most Influential | #PersonalBranding | #LinkedInLearning & #VengresoLive | FlyMSG.io | Vengreso.com

13

Customize Your Professional Headline

The section right under your name is your professional headline. Look at the branding you created from the first few tips in this book. You have 220 characters to describe who you help, how you help them, who you are and what you do. Try to utilize some of the keywords you have created in this section. Add emojis if relevant to your audience.

Type Less.
Sell More.

www.FlyMSG.io

Viveka (Vivica) von Rosen

Helping #SalesProfessionals Create More QUALIFIED & QUALITY Conversations | @LinkedInExpert & Speaker | Forbes Top 20 Most Influential | #PersonalBranding | #LinkedInLearning & #VengresoLive | FlyMSG.io

Name pronunciation +

 Your audio recording 

Visible to: All LinkedIn members

Headline

Helping #SalesProfessionals Create More QU...

Current position

Co-Founder | Chief Visibility Officer (CVO) |...

Add new position

14

From The Horse's Mouth

LinkedIn has a 10 second name pronunciation tool that allows you to record not only your name, but a mini elevator pitch. Conveniently, this feature is found right on top of your headline in the Intro section of your profile. Let people know your name, title, company and what you do. You can read that right from the headline. (At this time, you can only record on LinkedIn's mobile app.)

About

It's 2021 - And while things are starting to get a little more back on track, one thing remains. Virtual/ Remote selling is not going away. McKins ...see more

About

It's 2021 - And while things are starting to get a little more back on track, one thing remains. Virtual/ Remote selling is not going away. McKinsey shared an article that showed the pandemic has changed B2B Sales forever. Folks don't want to go back to the old way of endless site visits and field sales as it was. Is your sales team ready? Does your company have the brand and virtual selling skillset they need to dominate in this new world?

Is it a goal of your (mostly remote and virtual) sales team to win more business for your B2B company through #SocialSelling Strategies? We can help!

Vengreso is committed to one thing and one thing only, your sales success!

VENGRESO HELPS B2B COMPANIES REACH THE 90% OF BUYERS THAT CAN'T BE ACCESSED THROUGH TRADITIONAL OUTREACH.

WHO WE SERVE: Our approach has been customized for entrepreneurs and Fortune 50 companies alike.

WHAT WE DO: We provide digital sales strategies, tactics, and tools including personal branding, social selling training, and content for sales enablement, including:

👉 Content for Sales Enablement, so you have a blueprint for the messaging and content assets that meet the needs of your buyer at each stage of their journey - at scale

👉 Personal Branding, so that your LinkedIn pr
attracts your prospects from the get-go because

15

Start With A Call To Read

Start your About section with a "Call to Read". Meaning, your first sentence must get people to click on "See More". What question (other than "How much will this cost?") do your buyers always ask? You can state the question and answer in the first sentence. Or if you know your buyer has a common point of pain, state that and how you help.

Develop a standard for excellence.
Without distinction, there is extinction.
—Jon Michal, CEO Image International

16

Fill In Your About Section

Once people click on "See More," use the remaining 2000 characters to describe in more detail who you are, what you do, and whom you serve. Start with the paragraph pitch you've already written (Tip 7). Then use the buyer persona and the keywords you've created to speak to that perfect customer. Finish up with your contact info.

Background

Experience 

Vengreso | Award Winning Virtual Digital Sales Training
15 yrs 1 mo

Co-Founder | Chief Visibility Officer (CVO) | Master trainer | Head of Personal Branding
Full-time
2017 - Present · 4 yrs
California, Colorado, Florida, New Jersey, Indonesia, Colombia

As the Chief Visibility Officer and Master Trainer at Vengreso, it is my job to make sure that YOU know how to win more business using digital sales techniques like social selling. In particular, we teach you how to increase pipeline when
👉 #SellingWithLinkedIn
👉 #SellingWithSalesNavigator
👉 and #SellingWithVIdeo

♦ Are you a Sales or Marketing Leader who wants your sales team to:

⚫ Start more sales conversations with qualified buyers?
⚫ Grow their network of customer, prospects, and partners?
⚫ Connect with more decision makers through introductions and referrals?
⚫ Increase win rates by sharing insights?

We can help. As the world's largest Digital Selling Transformation company, we have helped Indust[illegible] / Sample Clients like:

Business Equipment - Hewlett Packard, Kyocera

17

Are You Experienced?

The Experience section on your profile is where you get to talk more about you and your company. You have 2000 characters to describe your company, what your company does, and what you do for the company. You can list services, features, and unique selling propositions here. Always highlight what makes you and your company different from everyone else.

Background

Education 

Wilfrid Laurier University 

Masters, Religion and Culture

Grade: 4.0

Activities and societies: Graduated with Honors, Graduate Student Teaching Assistant Liaison, co-created school’s recycling program, board member of GSA, Graduate Student Association, Student teacher, Native American Studies, Women's Studies

I spent considerable time on an Anishnabeg reservation in Northern Ontario, as well as interviewing, researching and writing the biography of Kiviaq (then known as David Ward) one of the first Inuit to be fully integrated into Caucasian Canadian culture.

Wilfrid Laurier University 

BA, English, Women's Studies
1987 - Jun 1990

Activities and societies: Graduated with Distinction

I was very involved in an Honor's English program and took additional classes in women's studies, psychology and philosophy.

Vengreso Selling with Social 

Selling with LinkedIn and Sales Navigator, LinkedIn
2019

Everything You Need to Know to “Sell” with Lin

18

Add Your Education

Whether you have your MBA from Harvard or a degree in the "Hard Knocks of Life," add your education to LinkedIn. It is part of who you are. You have 1000 characters to describe what you did in school and why it's relevant to who you are today. Even if what you studied is totally different from where you are today, add it. It speaks to your character.

Background

Licenses & Certifications

Selling with LinkedIn
Vengreso | Award Winning Virtual Digital Sales Training
Issued 2019 · No Expiration Date

See credential

Social Selling Boot Camp
Vengreso | Award Winning Virtual Digital Sales Training
Issued Mar 2017 · No Expiration Date
Credential ID 12109040

See credential

Inbound Marketing University
HubSpot
Issued 2009 · No Expiration Date

Social Media
Integrated Alliances
Issued 2006 · No Expiration Date

B2B LinkedIn Training
B2B LinkedIn LaunchPad Training Series

See credential

Show 5 more credentials

19

Get Certified

Let's face it. A lot of us have had a little extra time on our hands while #WFH during the pandemic. Why not use it to take a course or learn something new (LinkedIn Learning has lots of awesome authors and courses). And when you get your certification, share it on LinkedIn. Just add it to Background in "Add profile section."

9:37
◂ Search

Skills & Endorsements

Top Skills

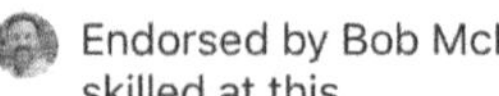

LinkedIn Training · 449

Endorsed by Bob McIntosh, CPRW, who is highly skilled at this

Endorsed by 2 of your colleagues at Vengreso | Award Winning Virtual Digital Sales Training

Digital Selling · 128

LinkedIn Speaker · 282

Industry Knowledge

Online Marketing · 1,127

Blogging · 1,258

Content Strategy · 215

Social Media Marketing · 1,475

Marketing Strategy · 595

Consulting · 281

Entrepreneurship · 651

Home My Network Post Notifications Jobs

20

List Your Skills

You can add up to 50 skills to your profile. If you don't yet have skills added, click on the drop-down beside "Add profile section." Choose the skills you want to highlight, otherwise LinkedIn might suggest skills you don't have. List your skills in the order you think is important and pin the top three to the top. Those will get the most endorsements (which will also help you get found).

It's important to build a personal brand because it's the only thing you're going to have. Your reputation online and in the business world is pretty much the same, so be a good person. You can't hide anything, and more importantly, you've got to be out there at some level.

—Gary Vaynerchuck, Influencer

21

Become More Findable

You want people to be able to find you by the keywords and skills associated with your brand. The more Skill Endorsements you have, the more findable you are on LinkedIn. The more you are known for something, the more likely it is you will be endorsed for it, and the more findable you become. To get more endorsements actively endorse others. And make sure you have your setting on to give and get endorsements

Accomplishments

54 PUBLICATIONS

Sales Hall of Fame
Badger Maps

19 HONORS & AWARDS

Sales Hall of Fame

16 PROJECTS

B2B Marketing on LinkedIn

← **Projects** +

B2B Marketing on LinkedIn

While LinkedIn—the world's largest and most powerful network of professionals—is widely recognized as a top recruiting tool, it also offers features that companies and individuals can leverage for business-to-business (B2B) marketing. In this course, join LinkedIn expert Viveka von Rosen as she shares best practices, tips, and strategies for effectively conducting B2B marketing on the LinkedIn platform. Viveka shares step-by-step actions that individuals on your sales team can take using video, updates, InMail, and other features. She also shares how to leverage Company Pages for B2B marketing, including how to best align marketing campaigns with LinkedIn, increase brand and culture awareness with video, and more.
Topics include:
Determining the right way to market your company on LinkedIn
Using long-form updates on your LinkedIn timeline
Expanding your network and business with InMail
SlideShare strategies that work
Aligning marketing campaigns with LinkedIn
Employee advocacy and Company Pages
Using sponsored updates and video

2018

See project

22

Add Your Projects

Whether you are an employee, entrepreneur, contractor or consultant, the Projects section allows you to share details about your work without having to list each and every one of the hundreds of jobs you've done in the Experience section. To add a project, click on the "Add profile section" button, and choose Projects under Accomplishments.

Accomplishments

54 PUBLICATIONS

Sales Hall of Fame
Badger Maps

Publications

Sales Hall of Fame

Viveka von Rosen - Sales Hall of Fame
Here at the Sales Hall of Fame, we honor some of the most distinguished professionals who continually inspire people with their cutting edge insights and intellectual influence.

Viveka von Rosen is co-founder and CVO (Chief Visibility Officer) of Vengreso. She is a contributor to LinkedIn's official Sales and Marketing blogs, and their "Sophisticated Marketer's" Guide. She is also a contributor to publications such as Fast Company, Forbes, Money, Entrepreneur, and The Social Media Examiner to name a few. Viveka uses the LinkedIn experience she has perfected over the past 10+ years and transforms it into engaging and informational training. Through her training, she has provided over 100,000 people with the tools and strategies they need to succeed on LinkedIn.

Need LinkedIn Advice? Start Here: https://www.linkedin.com/posts/linkedinexpert_salesleader-salesconversations-vengresopics-activity-6578371550330843136-P124/

For some more in depth best practices check out: www.PVCPlaybook.com

Check out Vengreso's training program: https://vengreso.com/digital-selling-with-linkedin-training-on-demand-online-course

23

Add Publications

Not everyone is a published author, but you may be a content creator. If you write a blog, have a podcast, publish a newsletter, have written an eBook, or use LinkedIn Articles, you are now considered a Publisher by LinkedIn. You don't want to list every piece of content you have ever created but do choose a few which really support your brand. As mentioned above, you can get to this from Accomplishments under "add profile section."

Successful technologies often begin as hobbies. Jacques Cousteau invented scuba diving because he enjoyed exploring caves. The Wright brothers invented flying as a relief from the monotony of their normal business of selling and repairing bicycles.

—Freeman Dyson

24

Add Your Organizations And Volunteer Work

Organizations you belong to and volunteer work you do both lend an emotional quality to your brand that helps to increase positive brand sentiment. Do consider leaving political and religious organizations out of this section - unless that IS your brand.

Viveka von Rosen

Contact Info 

Your Profile

linkedin.com/in/linkedinexpert

Websites

amazon.com/LinkedIn-Personal-Brand-network-business/dp/153710537X (Improve Your LinkedIn Brand!)

vengreso.com/our-team/viveka-von-rosen (Schedule some time with me!)

vengreso.com (Digital Sales Transformation)

Phone

877-483-6473 X7 (Work)

Email

viveka@vengreso.com

Twitter

LinkedInExpert

25

Add Your Contact Information

You can have the best brand in the world, but if you don't give people a way to contact you, it may not do you much good. Add your email address in the Contact section. If you add a phone number, consider adding a Google Voice number. You can hide your personal contact info (but then, what's the point?)

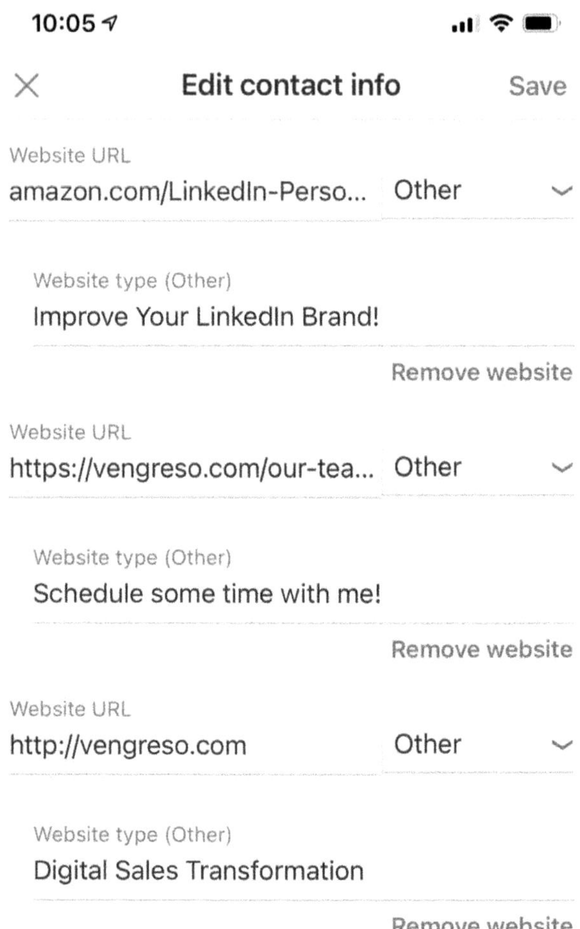
10:05
Edit contact info
Save
Website URL
amazon.com/LinkedIn-Perso...
Other
Website type (Other)
Improve Your LinkedIn Brand!
Remove website
Website URL
https://vengreso.com/our-tea...
Other
Website type (Other)
Schedule some time with me!
Remove website
Website URL
http://vengreso.com
Other
Website type (Other)
Digital Sales Transformation
Remove website

26

Customize Your Website Links

In Contact Info you can also add up to three URLs. Click "+Add website". When you edit your website, the dropdown menu gives you the option of "other." When you click on that, a new field opens that allows you to type in a description of the URL, (like "Improve Your LinkedIn Brand".)

Post with visuals drive up to 180% more engagement than those without.

—Ekaterina Walter, Author, Speaker, and Influencer

27

Add Branding Graphics

LinkedIn is becoming more visual. Pictures sell. If you are not a graphic artist, then invest in a graphic artist, use a freelancer or try out an online tool like Easil.com or Canva.com. The more visually professional your profile looks, the better you look.

Viveka (Vivica) von Rosen

Helping #SalesProfessionals Create More QUALIFIED & QUALITY Conversations | @LinkedInExpert & Speaker | Forbes Top 20 Most Influential | #PersonalBranding | #LinkedInLearning & #VengresoLive | FlyMSG.io | Vengreso.com

Vengreso | Award Winning Virtual Digital Sales Training · Wilfrid Laurier University

Loveland, Colorado, United States ·

500+ connections

Providing services

Public Speaking, Leadership Development, and Executive Coach...

See all details

Anyone

28

Use A Header Image

Upload a header or background image on your personal profile. Go to VengressoBanner.com for the latest dimensions. This is one of the easiest ways to emphasize your personal brand on LinkedIn. And it's not one and done. In the image above you will see a banner for FlyMSG.io, a software product we just launched. In a few weeks I'll go back to one of my Vengreso.com banners.

Visible to: Public

29

Add A Professional Profile Photo

This is not the place for a logo or your latest vacation photo. Use a photo that looks like someone your customers would want to do business with. How do you present yourself in front of customers on Zoom or in person? That's what you want here – a current, professional looking headshot.

Your profile picture validates who you are and supports the narrative that you are likeable, competent, and trustworthy.

—Guy Kawasaki, Author and Social Media Evangelist

30

This Century Please

The word "current" bears repeating here. When uploading your image, your headshot needs to look enough like you, so when you jump on Zoom, go to a conference, a trade show, or a job interview, you won't get blank stares due to a complete lack of recognition.

Googling yourself is not vain. It is a necessary tactic for managing your personal identity.

—Maya Demishkevich, Author

31

Google Yourself

Search your name, product, service – whatever your brand is – online. There may be videos or other media you can share. Keep the ones that are business or brand related. It is also a good way to find out if there is anything negative about you or your product or service online. Fix that ASAP.

Featured

Reorder

To all my entrepreneurs and sales people out there....... I have some important news!

We are changing the way Sales communicates and i...

Your Best Sales Productivity Tool

57 · 15 comments

★ Remove from featured

32

Get Featured

LinkedIn has a "Featured" section that will allow you to upload documents, share links or promote a post or article to highlight on your profile. This section is NOT "one and done" and should always be updated with the latest and greatest media you have. You can add featured media by clicking on the dropdown arrow of the "Add profile section".

Featured

See all

To all my entrepreneurs and sales people out there....... I have some important news!...

FlyMSG

Your Best Sales Productivity Tool

Type Less. Sell More.

57 · 15 comments

#LinkedInLive with Viveka von Rosen

Viveka von Rosen on LinkedIn

Check out my "Lives" listed below: How to Make Training Stick with Remote Selling...

12 · 1 comment

33

Add Video Links And Gifs

Just as graphics and photos are important to your profile, so are video and gifs. Video showcases your personality, your product, your service, and your admirers. Interviews, product demos, and testimonials add so much more to your profile – building credibility and showcasing your expertise. Add video as a YouTube or Vimeo link, or promoted Native video. If you add a gif to your featured Article, the movement is sure to catch the viewer's eye.

Viveka von Rosen

Helping #SalesProfessionals Create More QUALIFIED & QUALITY Conversa...

now •

Need a virtual speaker for your SKO next year? I'd love to chat with your sales team about how they can be making the most of LinkedIn and remote selling. Check out my Speaker's brief below for more info.

#vengresoevents
#KeynoteSpeaker
#SKO

   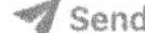

Like Comment Share Send

34

Utilize Slideshare Or Documents

Do you have a portfolio or a killer PowerPoint presentation? You can upload it to Slideshare and add a link to the presentation in an update or in your media sections (Featured and Experience). You can also upload it as a document in your posts/updates, which turns your PPT or PDF into a carousel of information.

The drawing shows me at a glance what would be spread over ten pages in a book.

—Ivan Turgenev

35

Add More Pictures

In addition to your professional headshot, add other photographs that brand you and your work. You can upload a picture of a project you have completed, an award you have won, a certificate you have received, or fascinating people you meet. Again, remember to keep those images professional. This is not the place to highlight your recent vacation.

10:09 

 Viveka von Rosen 

Got questions about Content for Sales? Digital Sales Transformation?
Contact us ✆ 877-4vengreso
✉ viveka@vengreso.com

Featured

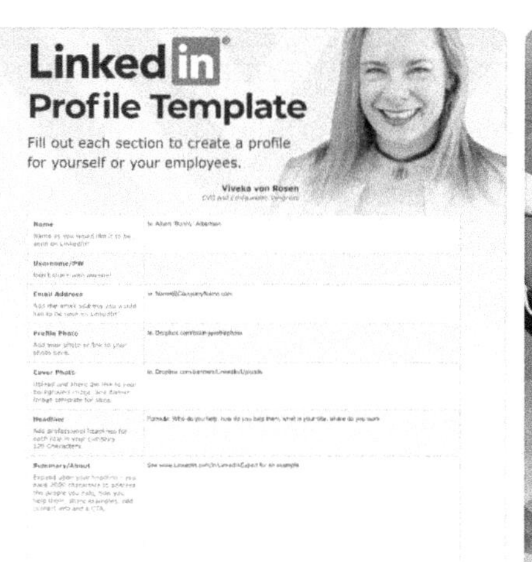

Download Your FREE LinkedIn Profile Template Here!

Vengreso - F
Methodolog

36

Add Additional Pdfs

Does your company have a brochure? Upload the PDF. Do you have a resume or a great cover letter? How about a chapter of your book? Take a section and upload it as a PDF. A word of advice - remove any personal contact information from your resume before you add the PDF.

Social Selling expands on the age-old basics of getting to know your customers and meeting their needs.

– Jon Ferrara, Nimble

37

A Word About Word

Word documents are great but always be careful with which ones you upload - anyone can download a Word document and make it their own.

Ask to be recommended

Received Given

" I wanted to drop the Vengreso team a quick thank you for helping us lift the bar of professionalism across our Australian based sellers in 2020, while also having a bunch of fun.

...see more

Jim Burke

Helping Businesses Flourish by bringing Unprecedented Simplicity, Reliability and Security to Enterprise Networks | Director of Sales | juniper.net

Dec 11, 2020, Jim worked with Viveka but at different companies

" I had the pleasure to have Viveka on the #stayhuman podcast! She was such an enthusiastic and engaging guest our conversation was incredible! Viveka is a true expert in her field and the way she shares information is admirable!

Malvina EL-Sayegh

#stayhuman sales|coaching|training

Aug 21, 2020, Malvina worked with Viveka but at different companies

38

Build Credibility With Recommendation

If there is someone you would like to recommend or get a recommendation from, make sure you are connected. To ask for a recommendation, go to your connection's profile and click on the More button, (or on mobile the three dots ...) From here you can ask for or give a recommendation.

The regular use of customer testimonials can help you generate roughly sixty-two percent more revenue not only from every customer but from every time they visit your brand.

—BigCommerce.com

39

Compose Your Own Recommendation

People are busy and will often ignore a request for a recommendation. Be thoughtful in any recommendations you give and help your friend out by giving them some talking points when requesting a recommendation. In your ask, add a sample of what you are looking for and say, "If this looks good to you, feel free to copy and paste into the recommendation."

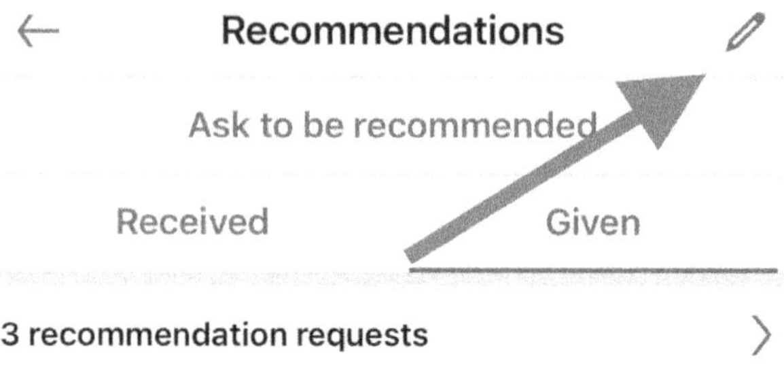

3 recommendation requests

" I can very much recommend not only guesting on- but listening to Malvina's podcast. She is a thoughtful and inquisitive host who manages to pull the most effective answers from her guests!

Malvina EL-Sayegh
#stayhuman sales|coaching|training
Jun 3, 2020, Viveka worked with Malvina but at different companies

" The reason I trust Sue B. Zimmerman when it comes to Instagram strategy is that she understands what it means to be intentional. Intentional with the brand she helps you to create, intentional with the content strategies she inspires and and intentional ...see more

Sue B Zimmerman
Instagram Expert | Social Media Educator & Consultant | Keynote and Breakout Speaker | Business Coach | #HuffPost Top 50
May 7, 2020, Viveka worked with Sue B but at different companies

40

Recommend Others

If you are not getting the recommendations you are asking for, then try recommending others on LinkedIn. Perhaps a nice recommendation will inspire them to recommend you. Never, ever ask or write recommendations for people you don't know or haven't worked with.

92% of customers read online reviews before buying

—Big Commerce

41

Using A Testimonial From Elsewhere

If you have a testimonial from someone, but you are not connected to that person on LinkedIn, find their profile and invite them to connect. Once connected, follow up with a message asking to use the testimonial as a recommendation. Copy and paste the whole testimonial in your request.

97% of B2B customers cited testimonials and peer recommendations as the most reliable type of content.

—Demand Gen Report

42

Repurposing Old Testimonials

If you have a stellar testimonial, but the author is not on LinkedIn (or won't connect to you) then you can always upload the testimonial as an image, as a PDF or even put a bunch of testimonials together in a Slideshare presentation. You can even copy and paste shortened testimonials right into the "Description" sections of your Summary, Experience, and Education.

In a world of endless spin, scandals, and something-gates, what people are really after is authenticity. They want to know what your goods or services are really like. Anything that smacks of corporate spin will backfire, writing off your testimonials as worthless or, worse yet, dishonest. The effectiveness of your testimonials is tied to how authentic users believe them to be.

—RocketSpark.com

43

Visual Testimonials

If a picture is worth a thousand words, imagine what a video testimonial is worth. It is too easy to shoot quality video these days with your phone – so no excuses. Get some video testimonials, upload them to YouTube or another video site, and add them to your profile.

A brand is simply trust.

—Steve Jobs, Apple

44

Get Endorsements

Endorsements are more of a Facebook "like" than a true testimonial to your awesomeness, but they still count. Make sure your Skills list is up to date, then endorse a few of your friends for their skills. Is your endorsement feature turned on? Remember, these endorsements make you more easily found on LinkedIn.

"Other than we're complete strangers," I said softly.

"Everyone is, until they aren't."

—Beau Brown, A Husband for Christmas

45

Buy Me A Drink First!

I'm going to make an assumption you wouldn't run up to someone at a live event, shove your business card in their face and ask them to buy your stuff. So why would you do that on LinkedIn? Just like in real life, you have to get to know someone a little bit first, before earning the right to ask for a meeting, phone call or zoom.

Personal branding is about managing your name—even if you don't own a business—in a world of misinformation, disinformation, and semi-permanent Google records. Going on a date? Chances are that your 'blind' date has Googled your name. Going to a job interview? Ditto.

—Tim Ferriss

46

First Things First

Before asking a complete stranger to connect with you, make sure to engage with them first. Find something on their profile, or in their activity you can respond to. The order SHOULD be: 1 - Build your brand, 2 - Find your prospects, 3 - Engage with your prospects, and only after you have done that, 4 - Reach out to connect.

The aim of marketing is to know and understand the customer so well the product or service fits him (or her) and sells itself.

—Peter Drucker, Author and Management Consultant

47

Search For Your Perfect Customer

Even if you are not in sales or marketing, you need the buyer persona you created earlier. The keywords, titles, and industries from that persona are a good place to start. LinkedIn won't let you search your network by economic qualifications, gender, or age. You can search by title, company, industry, keyword, name, school, and a variety of other free search fields.

in Search

Home My Network 37 Jobs

People Posts Jobs Companies Groups Schools Events All filters

Filter only **People** ▾ by

Connections

☐ 1st ☐ 2nd

☐ 3rd+

Connections of

+ Add a connection

Locations

☐ United States ☐ Colorado, United States

☐ Greater Fort Collins Area ☐ India

☐ Fort Collins, CO + Add a location

Reset **Show results**

48

Use "All Filters" When Searching For Connections

The additional search filters will help you refine your search. You'll get fewer search results, but they will be of higher quality and better potential to you. Click in the search box and then choose "People" from the dropdown. On the right you will see the option of "All Filters". Click on that to access the additional search options.

Good marketers see consumers as complete human beings with all the dimensions real people have.

—Jonah Sachs, Author

49

All Filter Search Criteria

All Filters will allow you to search by:

- Profile keywords like "entrepreneur" or "artistic"
- Titles such as "HR", "Consultant", "Job-seeker," or "CEO"
- Companies where key connections might work
- Schools your prospects have attended
- Cities where your connections live

Boolean searching is built on a method of symbolic logic developed by George Boole, a 19th century English mathematician. Boolean searches allow you to combine words and phrases using the words AND, OR, NOT (known as Boolean operators) to limit, broaden, or define your search.

– Shauntee Burns, Librarian

50

Use The Boolean Search Method

Currently, free members only get to see 100 search results (and sometimes less.) Using the Boolean qualifiers (AND, OR, NOT) will better sort your search results, organizing them in a logical way and more usable form as well as excluding those who don't meet your criteria for a prospect. Keep reading for usage tips and examples…

51

The Power Of "OR"

People use different words to describe themselves or their skills in their profiles. A business owner might call herself CEO, Managing Director, President, Founder, or Partner. Use a capitalized OR to include different titles for this search method such as: CEO OR "Chief Executive Officer" OR Owner OR President. (Quotation marks are used to hold words together in a search.)

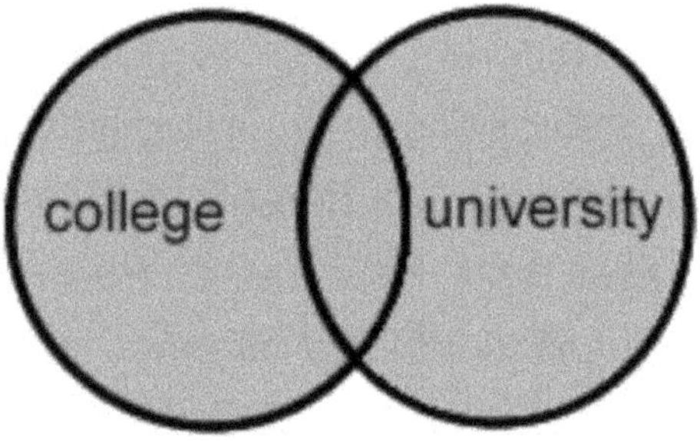

"OR" logic

OR : Using OR broadens a search to include results that contain either of the words you're looking for.

52

The Power Of "AND"

The use of AND refines your search when you want a specific term included in the search. For example: CEO OR "Chief Executive Officer" OR Founder OR Owner OR President AND beer AND microbrewery.

Note: In this type of search, AND is capitalized.

Absorb what is useful, reject what is useless,
add what is specifically your own.

—Bruce Lee

53

Not Gets Rid Of All The Riff Raff

As you have probably figured out, NOT excludes people from your search. Example: CEO OR "Chief Executive Officer" OR Founder OR Owner OR President AND beer AND micro-brewery NOT LinkedIn Expert NOT spammers NOT tomatoes. Capitalize NOT

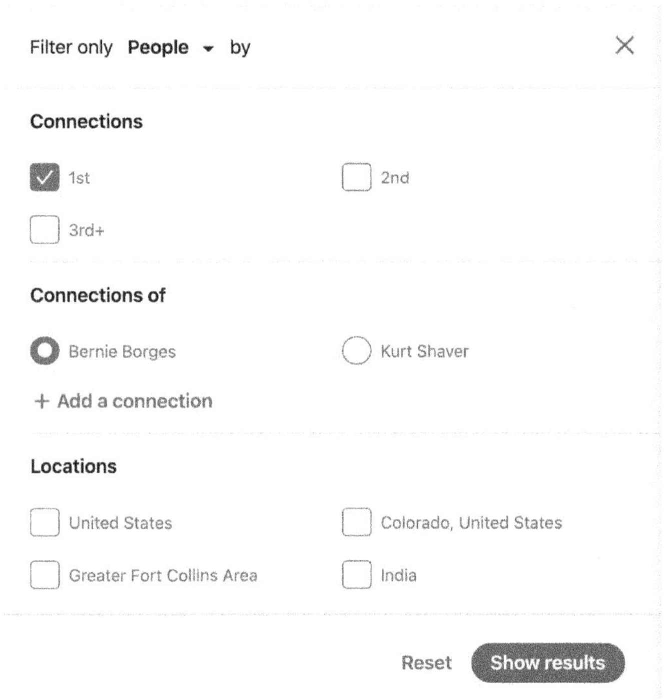

Filter only **People** ▾ by ✕

Connections

- [x] 1st
- [ ] 2nd
- [ ] 3rd+

Connections of

- (•) Bernie Borges
- ( ) Kurt Shaver

+ Add a connection

Locations

- [ ] United States
- [ ] Colorado, United States
- [ ] Greater Fort Collins Area
- [ ] India

Reset **Show results**

54

Searching Your Connections' Connections

To find the connections of your connections, click on the People search and then All Filters. In the middle you will see a field called "Connections Of". Type in the name of your first level connection to see their connections. You can use additional search fields as well.

"One and done" often refers to athletes who spend one year in college before moving on to professional sports. It's not great for basketball and it's not great for Boolean searches.

55

Create Your Search In A Word Document

Create your Boolean search in a Word document. This will catch spelling errors and allow you to see the whole search string. It makes changing the search much easier. Once you like your search words, pop the new string into the appropriate field and adjust as needed. This will also save you time when creating new searches, which you should do often, not "one and done."

No results found

Try removing filters or rephrasing your search.

Remove all filters Edit search

56

Zero Doesn't Always Mean Zero

If you get a "No results found" result, there is likely a spelling error in your search. The first step is to make sure there are no errors by checking your Word doc (or use Grammarly). If there are no errors, then sign out of LinkedIn and sign back in. Sometimes LinkedIn acts up. If you still get no results, try different search terms or expand your search.

If you don't give the market the story to talk about, they'll define your brand's story for you.

—David Brier

57

Save The Search Urls

You have already created your search in a Word (or Pages) doc, now you want to save the search URL to the same document. Just copy it from the browser and paste it into your document. This allows you to easily populate the search or share it with your employees or colleagues. If you create a perfect prospect search and send that URL to your employees, they can refine it via location, industry, etc.

Manage search alerts

Marketing NOT opportunities NOT secretary NOT assistant NOT consultant NOT LinkedIn (84 new)

Edit

Delete

Marketing NOT opportunities NOT secretary NOT assistant NOT consultant NOT LinkedIn NOT copywriter NOT recruiter NOT experienced (119 new)

facetValue · facetValue · facetValue and 6 more

Edit

Delete

Cancel

58

Save Your Search As An Alert Right On LinkedIn

You can save up to three search alerts with a free LinkedIn account, and more with a Premium or Sales Nav account. You must have a keyword in the search field as well as use some of the additional search fields to trigger an alert. LinkedIn will send you a weekly digest of new people who fall into that particular search algorithm.

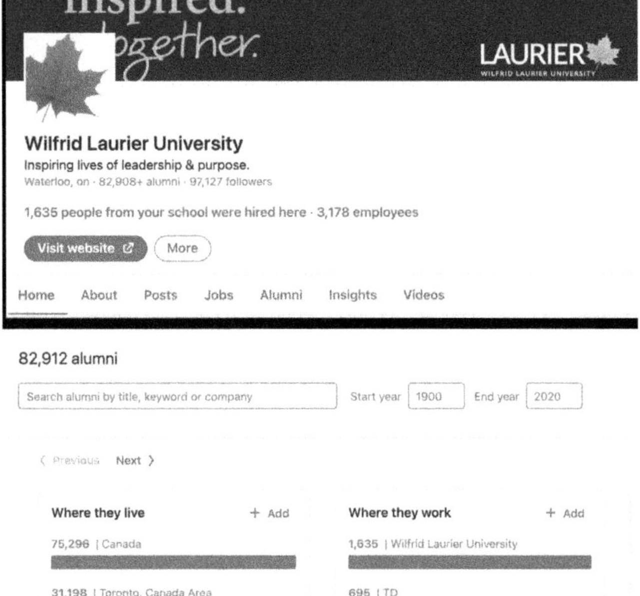
inspired.
together.
LAURIER
WILFRID LAURIER UNIVERSITY
Wilfrid Laurier University
Inspiring lives of leadership & purpose.
Waterloo, on · 82,908+ alumni · 97,127 followers
1,635 people from your school were hired here · 3,178 employees
Visit website
More
Home
About
Posts
Jobs
Alumni
Insights
Videos
82,912 alumni
Search alumni by title, keyword or company
Start year 1900
End year 2020
Previous
Next
Where they live
+ Add
75,296 | Canada
31,198 | Toronto, Canada Area
17,858 | Kitchener, Canada Area
6,575 | Ontario, Canada
Where they work
+ Add
1,635 | Wilfrid Laurier University
695 | TD
533 | Sun Life
522 | RBC
Show more

59

Searching For Alumni

If you want to find alumni, then instead of clicking on People in the search dropdown, just choose Schools. Once you find your school, click on the Alumni link. You will have the ability to further refine your search by keyword, year, location and company.

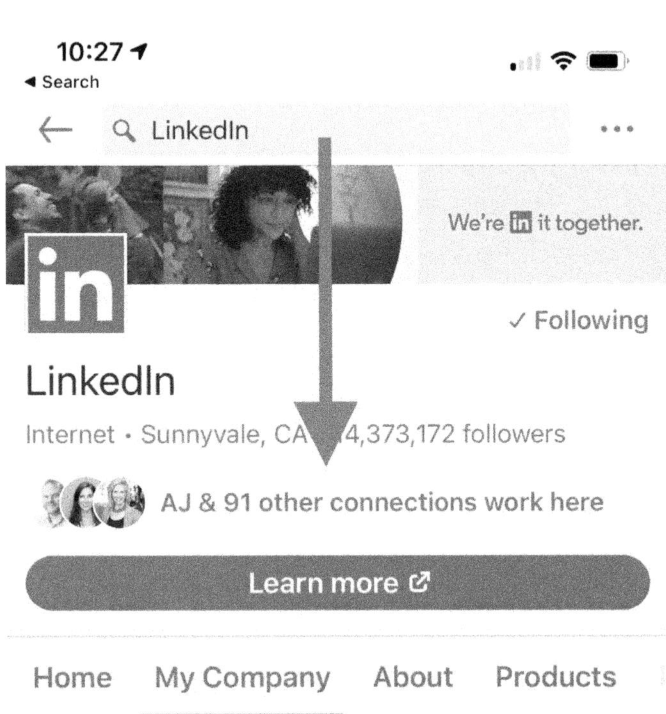
10:27
Search
LinkedIn
We're in it together.
✓ Following
LinkedIn
Internet • Sunnyvale, CA • 4,373,172 followers
AJ & 91 other connections work here
Learn more
Home
My Company
About
Products

60

Searching Companies

Search companies you would like to do business with. Choose the companies option in your initial search, and then on the Company Page, click on "Name and ## connections work here". From that page you can use the additional filters mentioned earlier.

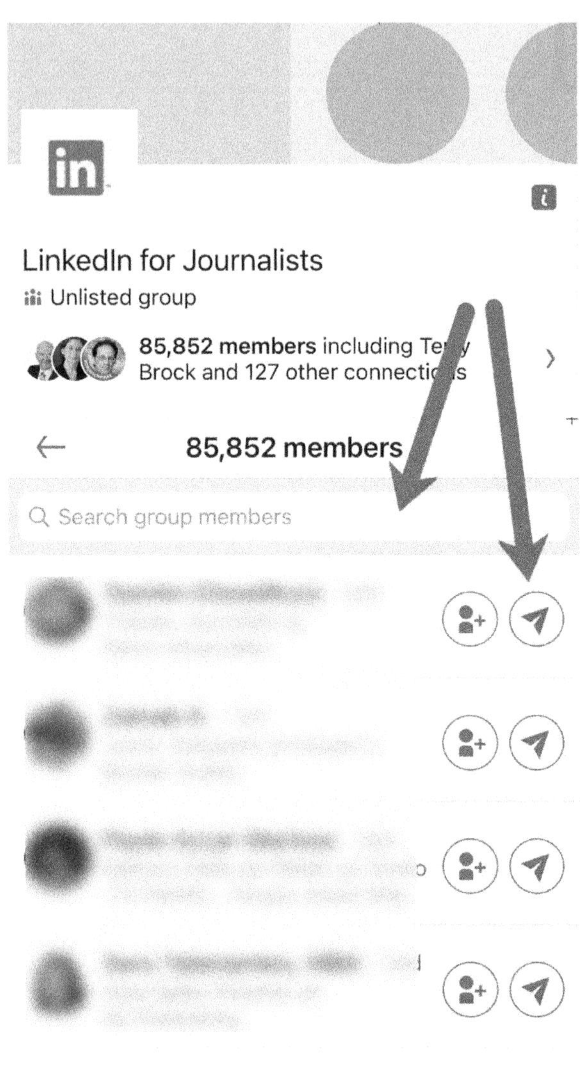
in
LinkedIn for Journalists
Unlisted group
85,852 members including Te y
Brock and 127 other connectio s
85,852 members
Search group members

61

Searching Groups

Groups are a good source for finding new connections because you already share something in common with other members – the group itself. Once you have joined a group, click on the “See All” members link. Now you can sort by name or keyword and send a message. Even if you are not connected.

Social is not a place for a hard sell – it's a place to build trust and credibility. Work the intelligence in to your formal sales process and messaging while staying top of mind by continuing to interact on a personal level over social media.

– Julio Viskovich

62

Engage First

Once you have found your prospect using the previous methods, the next step is engaging with them BEFORE inviting them to connect. Create name awareness so when you do reach out, they are more likely to accept your invitation.

← Articles, posts & more...

Bernie Borges
9,267 Followers

Following

ctivity | Articles | Posts | Documents | Int

Bernie Borges · 1st
Chief Customer Officer | Exceeding Expectations for B2B Sales and Marketin...
3m ·

#SalesManagers Now is the moment to participate in Vengreso's upcoming Sales Managers Guide that will be amplified through our extensive social ...see more

Sales Managers Guide - Calling All Sales Managers and Above - Submit your Best Pra...
d1tfz9268y8c5s.cloudfront.net

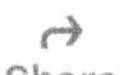

Like Comment Share Send

63

Engage On Their Content

Do a happy dance if your prospect is active on LinkedIn. Scroll down to their activity and check out the posts they are active on or sharing. You can like, comment and share their posts. You can comment on their comments in other people's posts.

Video in emails helps #sellers stand out from the competition, grabbing the prospect's attention while connecting more effectively with the viewer. For instance, video allows sellers to show empathy and emotion when communicating.

Learn more from Orechia's testimonial after attending Vengreso | Award Winning Virtual Digital Sales Training's Selling with Video Training program, who transformed a sales lead from cold to hot with a sales video message.

CHECK OUT HERE!

Sales Prospecting Tips: Sales Techniques for Finding Sales Leads Every Day

vengreso.com · 3 min read

 4 · 1 comment

What about... | Thank you for... | Very useful... | Love this.

Like  Comment Share Send

So true **Bernie**! Video messaging is a real differentiator. While of course you can send a video message natively on LinkedIn (using the mobile app), I prefer tools like **OneMob** for asset tracking.

64

Be An Engagement Ninja

If your prospect is sharing content (posts or articles) make sure to @mention them in your comments. Ask a question. Even upload an image or share a link. Your comment will stand out and will have a better chance of eliciting a response. After engaging on a few posts, then you can reach out and invite them to connect (and reference their post when you do so.)

Highlights

969 mutual connections

You and Bernie both know Anna Pleshakova, Cheryl Burgess, and 967 others

You both work at Vengreso | Award Winning Virtual Digital Sales Training and OneMob

Bernie started at Vengreso | Award Winning Virtual Digital Sales Training 7 years and 11 months after you did

Say hello

10 Mutual Groups

You and Bernie are both in Writing on LinkedIn, Content Marketing Academy (by Upland Kapost), and 8 others

How to Increase Sales Revenue and Maximize Business Success!

Bernie attended this event

Message

Show less ^

65

Deep Dive

Many times, your prospects won't be active on LinkedIn. You can still invite them to connect. Do a deep on their profile. What commonalities do you have? Did you go to the same school? Work in the same company? Did you find media they uploaded helpful? Use these similarities in your invitation.

Being introduced invites you into the conversation and makes you feel like part of the group. Making introductions is particularly important in business settings as they establish a rapport of respect, get relationships off on the right foot, and give you an aura of being confident, prepared, and in control.

—Bret and Kate McKay, The Art of Manliness

66

Inviting Connection's Connections

When you find one of more of your connections are connected to your prospects, do these two things. First, ask 2 or more of your mutual connections for an introduction. Choose your "best yes". Second, write the introduction for them and then ask them to CC you when they send it. (That way you'll know they did it AND you'll be able to communicate with your prospect and invite them to connect with you.)

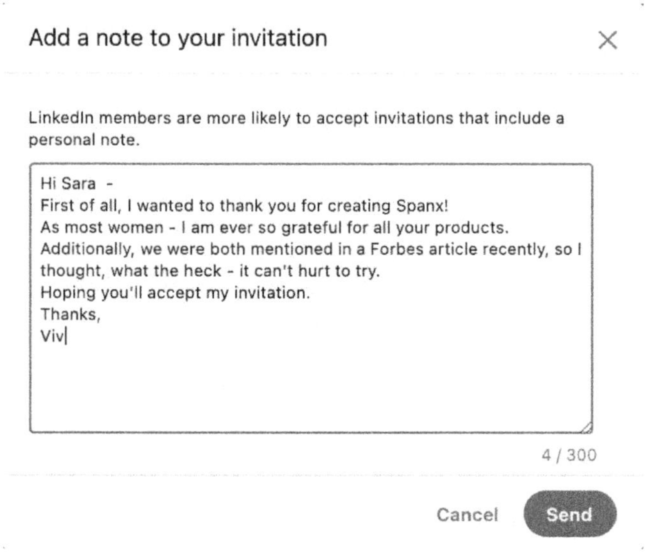

Add a note to your invitation

×

LinkedIn members are more likely to accept invitations that include a personal note.

Hi Sara -
First of all, I wanted to thank you for creating Spanx!
As most women - I am ever so grateful for all your products.
Additionally, we were both mentioned in a Forbes article recently, so I thought, what the heck - it can't hurt to try.
Hoping you'll accept my invitation.
Thanks,
Viv

4 / 300

Cancel **Send**

67

Sending A Customized Invitation

Always, always, always customize your invitation when you can. (Occasionally a LinkedIn member will turn off this feature.) On mobile, click on the three dots … OR click on More and "Personalize" invite. You have 300 characters to customize the invitation.

You don't build a business – you build people – and people build the business.

—Zig Ziglar, Author and award-winning salesman

68

Be Conservative About Who You Reach Out To

Don't go crazy and invite everyone to join your network. You are limited to 5000 invitations, and a total network of 30,000. In addition, if too many people say they don't know you (an IDK) LinkedIn might restrict your account. This is yet another reason why sending a customized invite is so important.

69

Pay For It

If you are in sales, or find your searches, invitations and messaging restricted by LinkedIn, you might consider Sales Navigator. One of LinkedIn's premium accounts, it has more search fields, endless search results and 15 saved search alerts. Not to mention the ability to save leads and create leads lists to track them. (As well as numerous other benefits.)

4:48

Jo Saunders
Active now

Jo 2021 prediction.mp4
dropbox.com • 1 min read

MONDAY

Jo Saunders • 8:05 am
Thanks Viveka
Thats great!

You're welcome
Cool

Write a message...

Attachment Photos Camera Video

GIF

GIF Mention

70

Getting Your Message Across

You can share private messages on LinkedIn. It's one of the best ways for you to develop relationships through personal engagement. You can now add voicemail on Mobile as well as video messages, pictures, gifs, schedule a zoom call and even add your calendar for scheduling.

If your stories are all about your products and services, that's not storytelling. It's a brochure. Give yourself permission to make the story bigger.

—Jay Baer, Author, Speaker, and Influencer

71

Messaging Via The 80/20 Rule

Unless your brand is being a spammy spambot, then only use LinkedIn Messenger to share information and content your prospects and clients would be interested in. Don't spam your brand new connections with your free webinar or pitch for your new product. After a few messages back and forth, you can ask for a phone call or a meeting.

72

Proper Use Of Inmail

InMails are paid messages you can use to send private messages to people who are NOT your first level connections. They can be very effective when used to get to know someone. They are not at all effective if you are blasting a bunch of sales messages or recruiting messages to people who neither know, like, nor trust you yet. InMail will cost you $10 a pop if you have the free account, and you get 10 – 25 free with premium accounts. Use these only as a last resort.

I've learned that people will forget what you said, people will forget what you did, but people will never forget how you made them feel.

—Maya Angelou, Author and Poet

73

Share More Updates

Sharing even one update a week will increase the visibility of your profile. Once a day is even better. Your profile is your brand; so increased visibility will increase your prospects' sense of knowing, liking, and trusting you, which leads to increased business.

Viveka von Rosen
Helping #SalesProfessionals Create More QUALIFIED & QUALITY Convers...
4d ·

The average tenure of a #sales rep is 15 months and replacing them costs organizations $97,690 on average. That's why when building sales teams, sales #leaders must know how to attract, develop and retain top talent. ...see more

Building Sales Teams: How to Attract, Develop and Retain Top Talent, with Wendy Mitchell-Covington, Episode #145

vengreso.com · 3 min read

9 · 2 comments

Like Comment Share Send

330 views of your post in the feed

74

Curated And Created Content

You can share content you create such as a blog post, a YouTube video, a podcast link or a document. And, you can also curate content (share other people's content you find interesting) you think your network might benefit from. Both options build your KLT factor (know, like and trust).

Viveka von Rosen

Helping #SalesProfessionals Create More QUALIFIED & QUALITY Conve...

11mo • Edited •

Hey #SocialSeller and #SocialMarketers

If you have a great marketing asset to share, be it an instructional video (like this one), an informational infographic or presentation, or a link to your company's latest post, make sure to apply the steps below in order to get the most visibility and activity!

The Anatomy of a Good LinkedIn Post

1. Choose an asset to share (Link, Document, Image/Video)
2. Address your targeted audience
3. Describe the asset (what it's about, what's in it, etc.)
4. Use emojis for visual interest
5. Tag relevant LinkedIn members or companies
6. Use 3 industry hashtags and 1 unique one
7. Add a CTA
8. Promote with a sharing hub

If you create a long-form post using the steps above, make sure to share it in the comments below!

And for more great info like this, check out all our Vengreso resources https://lnkd.in/ejrWfaN

#VengresoVids
#SellingwithLinkedIn
#SocialSelling
#SocialVideo
#SocialVideoSelling

75

The Anatomy Of A Good Post

When sharing content, don't just add the link and click on share. You have 1200 characters to let your network know what's in the media you are sharing and why they should read it. Add emojis to attract the human eye, bullets and numbers lists for easier consumption, and @ Mention relevant people or companies.

Either write something worth reading or do something worth writing about.

—Benjamin Franklin

76

Hashtags

Hashtags are a thing again on LinkedIn. Use them in your posts to make your content more visible and findable. You can use popular hashtags (#SocialMedia), niche hashtags (#SellingWithLinkedIn) and unique hashtags (#VengresoPics). Use between 3-6 in every post.

Viveka von Rosen | Linked...
281 followers
3mo •

+ Follow

Do you want to look more famous on LinkedIn? Then change your Connect button to a Follow button by following these 3️⃣ easy steps!

1️⃣ ON LinkedIn's MOBILE 📲 app, go to your settings.
2️⃣ Get to settings by clicking on home 🏠 icon, then the image of yourself on the top left, then the View Profile link, then the Settings ⚙️ icon
3️⃣ In Privacy scroll down to "Who Can Follow You" and turn on "Make follow primary"

Watch the video below to see how!

PS - I was just told you can also access it on Desktop in Privacy Setting under Blocking and Hiding. Naturally, I don't have that option - but you might!!!!

PPS - This will hide the Connect button in your "more" section, so might decrease the number of invitations you get (which could be a good or bad thing!) So decide if you want to be easier to connect with or have more followers!

#VengresoVids
#LinkedInTips

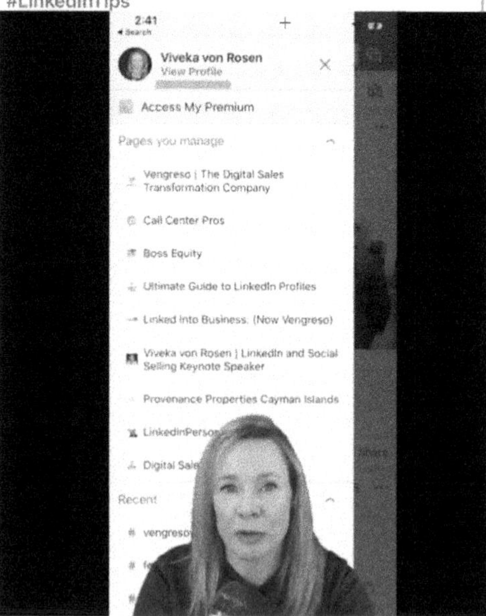

77

Native Video

If you really want to build your brand on LinkedIn, consider using Native Video. You can shoot and upload video to LinkedIn (under 10 minutes and 5 gigs.) You can do a product demo, upload a testimonial, do a book review or a quick interview. Generally, the shorter the better (between 15 and 90 seconds.)

Do or do not; there is no try.

—Yoda

78

LinkedIn Live

You can apply on LinkedIn for LinkedIn Live. This gives you the opportunity to Livestream to your personal or Company page. #LinkedInLive is an awesome way to interview industry leaders, share your knowledge, showcase your company or product and services and position yourself as a thought leader in your own right.

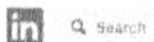

Create a LinkedIn Page

Connect with clients, employees, and the LinkedIn community. To get started, choose a page type.

Small business
Fewer than 200 employees

Medium to large business
More than 200 employees

Showcase page
Sub-pages associated with an existing page

Educational institution
Schools and universities

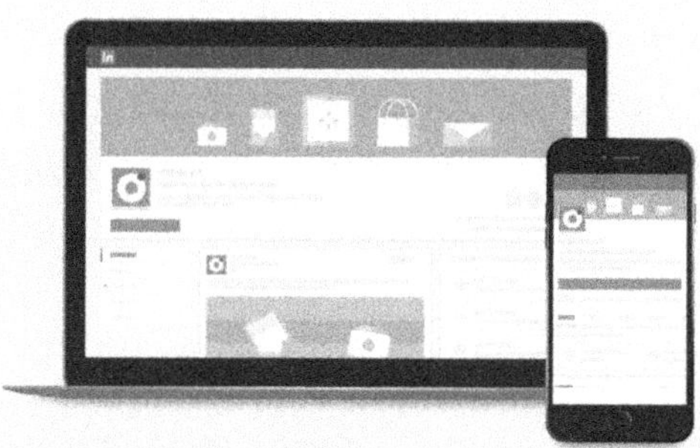

79

Creating A Company Page

According to LinkedIn, over 80% of the 720+ million members want to connect with Company Pages. Create your Company by clicking the "Create a company page" link in the Work grid. Or go to https://www.linkedin.com/company/setup/new/. You will need a unique website for your email address (name@companyname.com)

Vengreso | Award Winning Virtual Digital Sales Training

Home About Posts Jobs People Insights Events Videos

Overview

The modern buyer requires a modern seller...

Fact - all salespeople want more conversations with qualified buyers!

Vengreso is the first company to deliver a full suite of digital sales training and consulting services helping B2B sales teams create more conversations with qualified buyers through three solutions:

1. Content for Sales Enablement
2. LinkedIn Profile Makeovers
3. Digital Sales Training and Coaching

The modern salesperson creates more conversations that can lead to more wins:

- content that is relevant to their buyer
- a distribution channel to deliver content
- a LinkedIn profile written through the lens of the buyer
- skills to find, engage, connect and feed their network

Vengreso's award-winning 10 Step Digital Selling Program is unlike any other and proven to drive 100% sales rep adoption of your digital sales processes and tools.

Website: https://vengreso.com

Resources:
https://vengreso.com/ultimate-guide-to-linkedin-profiles-sales-professionals
https://vengreso.com/resources/digital-selling-benchmark-report
https://vengreso.com/cold-calling-vs-digital-prospecting
https://vengreso.com/resources/selling-power
https://www.youtube.com/c/Vengreso

Join the (digital sales transformation) movement!

877-483-6473

Website https://vengreso.com

80

Word Again

Start with a Word document as you did before. Copy and paste the About section from your company website as the foundation for your new company page description. Customize it specifically for LinkedIn with an opening message or "call to read." As you did with your personal summary, use white space, special characters, bullets, and capitalization to enhance this description.

Home About Posts Jobs People In

Specialties	LinkedIn Company Profile Optimization, Social Media Marketing, LinkedIn Marketing and Consulting, LinkedIn Professional Profile Optimization, LinkedIn Corporate Training, LinkedIn Group Creation and Strategy, Social Selling, Digital Sales, Digital Selling, Social Seling Training, Digital Sales Training, Digital Video Training, Social Selling Coaching, Sales Training, Content Marketing, Sales and Marketing Alignment, Employee Advocacy, Social Media Strategy, LinkedIn Training, Lead Generation, Twitter Training, Sales Pipeline, Sales Funnel Development, Content Marketing Strategy, LinkedIn Profile Makeover, LinkedIn Profile Optimization, Content Creation, Blog Writing, LinkedIn Profile Writing, LinkedIn Profile Writer, Social Video, LinkedIn Training, LinkedIn for Sales Trainers, LinkedIn Coaching, Social Media Classes, LinkedIn Workbook, Sales Trainer Programs, Social Video Training, Digital Sales

81

Keywords And Findability For Your Company

If relevant, use the same keywords you created for your personal profile in your company page description. You have up to 2000 characters to describe your company, as well as up to 20 specialties you can add for findability.

Vengreso | Award Winning Virtual Digital Sales Training

Start more sales conversations - fill your pipeline NOW! #ModernSelling

Professional Training & Coaching
Walnut Creek, CA • 9,602 followers

Mario & 37 other connections work here

Learn more

Home About Posts Jobs People

82

Add A Company Page Image

This is a real opportunity to create visually arresting images that grab a viewer's attention and get the visitor to scroll down to your updates. Download the template at www.VengresoBanner.com. Consider creating Personal Profile Banners that match your company banner branding. And don't forget to change them up for special events, product launches, holidays, etc.

Vengreso | Award Winning Virtual Digi...
9,602 followers
23h •

WOW! Our show "The Modern Sales Mastery Show" is in The Sales Experts Channel

Hosted by our founders, Mario Martinez, Jr., Kurt Shaver and Viveka von Rosen.

It is the go-to show for everyone responsible for generating #revenue. The show inspires you to create more #sales conversations with your target buyer.

Join the show every Tuesday, 11 AM PT, here
https://hubs.ly/H0D7BwD0

#SalesMethodology #SalesProductivity #SalesTraini

Like

Comment

Share

Send

83

Company Page Updates

Your Company Page update has similar function to your personal profile, so use the same "Anatomy of a Good Post." It's OK to use the same post on your personal page and company page OR you can post it to your company first and then share to your personal page. In most cases, your personal posts will get more engagement.

The nice part about employee advocacy is that it actually shrinks the distance between the brand and the customer, but at the same time it allows the brand to reach more people and have a much more humanized voice.

—Brian Fanzo, Founder & CEO, iSocialFanz

84

Encourage Engagement On Your Company Page

Anyone on LinkedIn can comment on, like, or share a company status update - when they do, their network also sees the post. Share your Company page updates more than once a week on your personal feed as well as encouraging employees to do the same. Send a weekly email to your employees with links to the updates you want shared or simply use the "Notify Employees" link at the top of your post.

Marketing Solutions 

Reach target customers and generate leads with Sponsored Content

Run native ads in the LinkedIn feed across desktop and mobile

Create ad

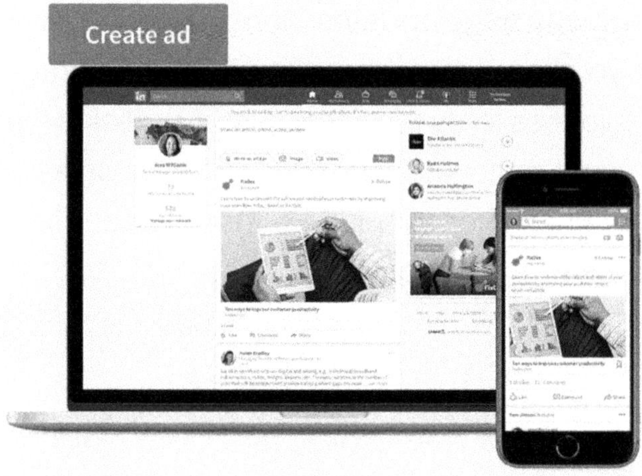

85

Sponsored Posts

A sponsored post is when you pay to get your Update seen by more people who are not in your network and do not follow your company page. To get the most bang for your effort, sponsor (pay for) updates that are already doing well. Sponsoring even one or two of the updates will increase the likelihood your posts in the series will be seen, read, and amplified by your growing network of followers.

Jobs People Insights Events Videos

Upcoming events

Vengreso | Award Winning Virtual Digital Sales Training has no upcoming events planned

Past events

Standout Virtual Events with David Meerman Scott in this #VengresoLive

Dec 18, 2020, 9:30 AM - 10:00 AM (your local time)

Online event

Andrea Higuita Caro, Bryan Vinarao and 77 other attendees

Manage event Share

Creating B2B Content for Sales Enablement Strategies - Ardath Albee

Dec 11, 2020, 9:30 AM - 10:00 AM (your local time)

Online event

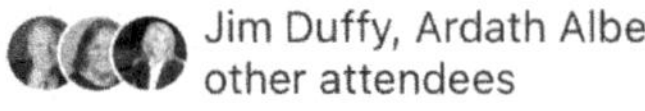

Manage event Share

86

Create A LinkedIn Event

From your LinkedIn Page's Admin tab, you can create a virtual or in person event invitation, including the event name, broadcast link (if it's a LinkedIn Live event), time and date, event description and even ticketing website. Once the event is created, you can invite people to join it by sharing the link to your followers.

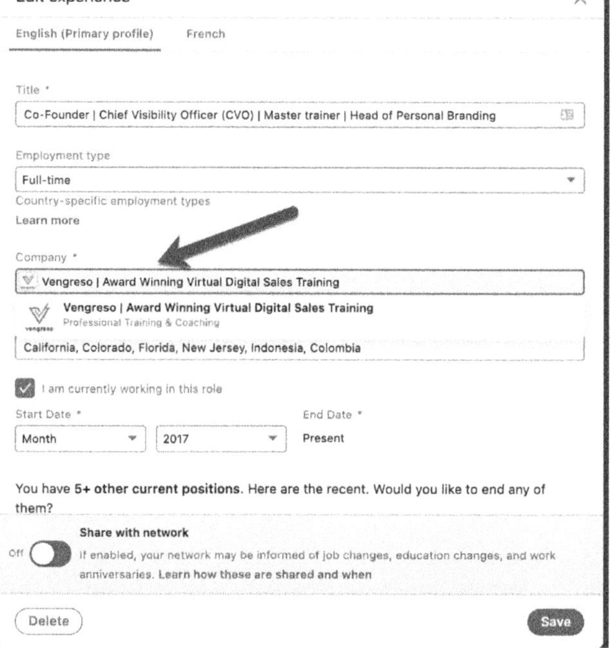
Edit experience
English (Primary profile)
French
Title *
Co-Founder | Chief Visibility Officer (CVO) | Master trainer | Head of Personal Branding
Employment type
Full-time
Country-specific employment types
Learn more
Company *
Vengreso | Award Winning Virtual Digital Sales Training
Vengreso | Award Winning Virtual Digital Sales Training
Professional Training & Coaching
California, Colorado, Florida, New Jersey, Indonesia, Colombia
I am currently working in this role
Start Date *
Month
2017
End Date *
Present
You have 5+ other current positions. Here are the recent. Would you like to end any of them?
Share with network
Off
If enabled, your network may be informed of job changes, education changes, and work anniversaries. Learn how these are shared and when
Delete
Save

87

Branding Across Employees' Profiles

Ask employees to connect their profiles to your Company page. Have employees add or edit their existing Experience section, choosing your company from the dropdown menu to connect to your Company Page. This has the added benefit of creating a navigation link and embedding your logo on their personal profiles. This serves to amplify your Company page.

Your personal brand is what people say about you when you are not in the room – remember that.

—Chris Ducker

88

Join Strategic Groups

Join LinkedIn groups in your own market or industry, your ideal client's industry, groups you are interested in, groups your target prospects are members of, alumni groups, and/or your own company's group. Once you join a group, you can send messages to strategic members and prospects (up to 15 a month in ALL your groups total) or invite strategic members to connect with you.

It doesn't matter how the paint is put on, as long as something is said.

—Jackson Pollack, Artist, Innovator, and Disruptor

89

Create A Group

Consider creating a Group on LinkedIn. Task someone in the group or in your company to moderate it in order to keep it interesting and relevant. Make your group a destination by keeping it a current and active forum.

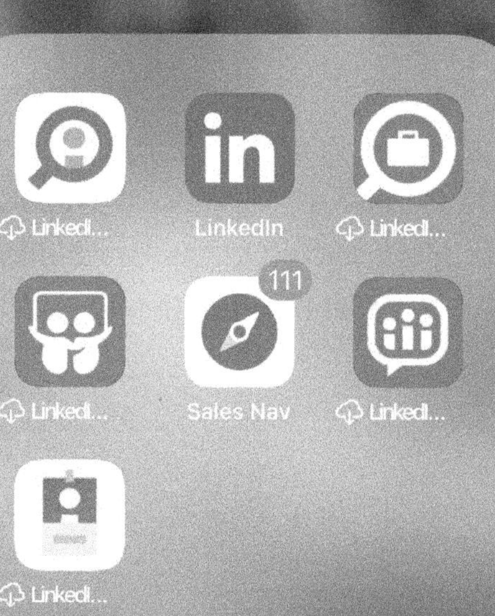
LinkedIn AppsIMG_9672.J...
LinkedI...
LinkedIn
LinkedI...
LinkedI...
111
Sales Nav
LinkedI...
LinkedI...

90

Be Mobile With LinkedIn

Build your brand on the fly using the LinkedIn mobile app. Take a picture and share it as an update. Are you at a conference and realize your profile has your old position listed as your current job? Or there's a blaring spelling error? No problem. You can now edit (most) of your profile from your mobile LinkedIn app. Invite people to connect. Send a voicemail or video message. There's so much you can do with the LinkedIn Mobile app.

Marketing is never done. It's about perpetual motion. We must continue to innovate every day.

—Beth Comstock, Author

91

Manage And Maintain Your Inbox

Just as you do with your email, keep on top of your LinkedIn inbox in a timely manner. You don't want to miss important connections, messages, and new prospects.

To: Dayna Steele

Cc/Bcc, From: vivekavr@gmail.com

Subject: LinkedIn book images

Chat soon!

Viveka von Rosen
Chief Visibility Officer & Co-founder at Vengreso

P 877-483-6473 x704 **M** 970-481-8916
E viveka@vengreso.com
W https://vengreso.com
Skype Linked.Into.Business

Schedule a free 15-minute meeting with me

92

Add LinkedIn To Your Email Signature

Add your customized LinkedIn link to your email signature. If you have a Company or Group page, add those links as well. A call to action with your signature - *Let's connect on LinkedIn* - works well too. There are many free online tools, such as WiseStamp, that create professional email signatures with embedded social links across most mail services.

93

Add LinkedIn To Your Website

If you have a website, add your LinkedIn customized URL link and/or your Company page link. There are several plugins to choose from that will do it for you. Search LinkedIn Company Page Plugin to get an embed code. Or ask your web developer to add one for you. And make sure it points to the right page!

 Edit your custom URL

Personalize the URL for your profile.

www.linkedin.com/in/linkedinexpert 

 Public Profile badge

Promote your profile by adding a badge to your blog, online resume, or website.

Create a badge

94

Add LinkedIn To Your Business Card

Add your customized LinkedIn URL to your business cards. Business card companies (like Vistaprint) have the option of adding your social info and populate it with the appropriate social icon. If you change your customized link in the future, don't forget to change it on your cards.

A brand is no longer what we tell the consumer it is - it is what consumers tell each other it is.

—Scott Cook, Co-Founder of Intuit

95

Share Across Social Media Platforms

Share your personal, company, and LinkedIn group links across all your social media sites. Give potential connections a reason why they should connect with you – great information, discounts, important updates, etc. Share those links a few times a month, just to let people know where you are active.

The successful networkers I know, the ones receiving tons of referrals and feeling truly happy about themselves, continually put the other person's needs ahead of their own.

—Bob Burg

96

Send A Personal Email To Your Network

Compose a message to your email list letting them know about your updated LinkedIn profile or your new LinkedIn group and/or Company page. As always, let your network know why they should connect with you or follow your Company page and/or Group. Mention you will be sharing resources, promos, events, and a community they will not be able to find anywhere else.

11:03
◂ App Store

Viveka von Rosen

Sort by ▾ Type ▾ Level ▾ Time to Comple

COURSE
B2B Marketing on LinkedIn
6m 51s left

COURSE
Employer Branding on LinkedIn
41m left

COURSE
HTML Essential Training
Ken Lantz likes this

COURSE
Writing a Press Release
Andrew Edsall likes this

COURSE
Writing Headlines
14,051 viewers

COURSE
Magento Community Edition 2 Essential Training
9,057 viewers

LEARNING PATH

My Learning Recommended Topics

97

LinkedIn Learning

LinkedIn Learning is an amazing premium resource. It offers over 16000 courses on everything from Apple watch tips to learning how to fly a drone to B2B Marketing with LinkedIn (spoiler – that's one of my courses.) It's included in most premium accounts or can be purchased for $29/mos.

Scheduling is the art of planning your activities so that you can achieve your goals and priorities in the time you have available.…Time is the one resource that we can't buy, but we often waste it or use it ineffectively. Scheduling helps you think about what you want to achieve in a day, week or month, and it keeps you on track to accomplish your goals.

—MindTools

98

Schedule Your Time

This is not only true for LinkedIn, but very useful for social media in general. If you create a schedule you are more likely to stick to it. Unless something is urgent or extremely timely, set days and times that work best for you. Keep a file of things you would like to share when it comes time to update on LinkedIn.

Linked in
LinkedIn Action Checklist

99

Create A Checklist

Create a checklist of daily, weekly, monthly and one-time only actions. Daily actions should include reaching out to your best connections and sharing posts as well as responding to messages, people who have viewed your profile or have commented on or shared your posts or updates. Every week you should write a post and connect to new prospects. Every month you should do a quick review of your profile and make sure it's up to date.

11:04

◂ Search

agorapulse

Manage your social media profiles on the go!

Sign in with email

You **must have** an Agorapulse account to start using the app.

Terms of service - Privacy policy

100

Delegate Or Schedule What You Can

If you are lucky enough to have an assistant, delegate what you can. (LinkedIn is cracking down on other people signing into your account, so you might have to use a VPN or screenshare.). Also, post scheduling tools like AgoraPulse and Hootsuite are great tools that will save you time as well.

Branding demands commitment; commitment to continual re-invention; striking chords with people to stir their emotions; and commitment to imagination. It is easy to be cynical about such things, much harder to be successful.

—Sir Richard Branson

101

Follow The Golden Rule

Do unto others as you would have them do unto you. LinkedIn is about branding, engaging, connecting and creating real relationships, in a consistent manner. Do more than sell and advertise all the time. Instead, share valuable information, answer questions, share others' updates, or pass on new job information. Remember, on LinkedIn or anywhere, the more you give, the more you get!

Be yourself. Everyone else is taken.

—Oscar Wilde, Author

Daily Success
THE BOOK SERIES